ABIGAIL

The Quilt Story

by Tony Johnston

pictures by Tomie dePaola

G. P. Putnam's Sons

New York

For Ann Doherty Johnston,
who taught me the joy of quilting
T J

For Nannie, Jill and Becca
T DEP

Text copyright © 1985 by Tony Johnston. Illustrations copyright © 1985 by Tomie dePaola.
All rights reserved. This book, or parts thereof, may not be reproduced in any form without
permission in writing from the publisher. G. P. Putnam's Sons, a division of
The Putnam & Grosset Book Group, 200 Madison Avenue, New York, NY 10016. First Sandcastle
Books edition, 1992. Sandcastle Books and the Sandcastle logo are trademarks belonging to
The Putnam & Grosset Book Group. Designed by Nanette Stevenson. Published simultaneously
in Canada. Printed in Hong Kong by South China Printing Co. (1988) Ltd.
Library of Congress Cataloging in Publication Data.   Johnston, Tony.   The quilt story.
SUMMARY: A pioneer mother lovingly stitches a beautiful quilt which warms and comforts
her daughter Abigail; many years later another mother mends and patches it for her
little girl.   1. Children's stories, American.   [1. Quilts—Fiction.
2. Quilting—Fiction.   3. Mothers and daughters—Fiction.]   I. dePaola, Tomie, ill.
II. Title.   PZFJ6478Qu 1984   [E]   84-18212
ISBN 0-399-21009-1 (HC)
9   10
ISBN 0-399-22403-3 (Sandcastle)
3   5   7   9   10   8   6   4   2

A little girl's mother
made the quilt
to keep her warm
when the snow came down,
long ago.

She stitched the quilt
by a yellow flame,
humming all the time.
She stitched the tails of
falling stars.
And she stitched the name,
Abigail.

Abigail loved the quilt.
She wrapped it round her
in the quiet dark
and watched the winter skies.
Sometimes she saw a falling star.

So her mother stitched it up

once more.

Sometimes she played
hide-and-seek
with her sisters.
She laughed and cried, "Don't peek!"
and hid under the quilt.
And everyone found her.

Sometimes Abigail was sick.

She sneezed and sneezed.

Then she slept under the quilt.

And she felt better.

One day Abigail's family moved away,
across wide rivers
and over a rock-hard trail.

The quilt went too.
Not stuffed in trunks with
the blankets and clothes.
It kept the little girls
warm from the wild winds.
Warm from the rain.
Warm from the sparkling nights.

They built a new house
in the woods.
Abigail's father built it
with his hatchet,
chop, chop, chop.
He built her a new bed,
chip, chip, chip.

He made her a new horse too.
He worked until curly shavings
covered the floor
and everyone sneezed and said,
"Welcome home," and was glad.
And Abigail felt sad.

New house. New horse. New bed.
Everything smelled of
fresh chops and chips.
Everything but the quilt.

So her mother rocked her
as mothers do.
Then tucked her in.
And Abigail felt at home again
under the quilt.

One day when the quilt
was very old and very loved,
Abigail folded it carefully
and put it in the attic.
Everyone forgot it was there.

A grey mouse came
and loved the quilt.
Her babies were born
on top of it.
They grew fat and grey in the warm stuffing.
When they got hungry,
they ate a falling star.

A raccoon came
and loved the quilt.
She dug a hole in a corner
with her black paws
and hid an apple there.

A cat came
and loved the quilt.
A patchwork cat.
It rolled on the stars,
and stuffing spilled out like snow.
Then the cat curled up in the snow
and purred.

"Kitty, Kitty," called a little girl.
She found her cat,
and she found the quilt,
splashed with patterns of sun.

The little girl wrapped the quilt
round her.
And she loved it too.

"Can you make it like new?"
she asked her mother.

So her mother patched the holes.
She pushed fresh stuffing in.
She stitched long tails on the stars
to swish
across the quilt again.

One day the little girl's family moved away,
across miles and miles
of pavement
and snaking grey highways.

They found a new house.

Freshly cleaned.

Freshly waxed.

Freshly painted. White.

They unpacked and unpacked.
All night.
And everyone sneezed on cardboard dust
and said, "Welcome home," and was glad.
And the little girl felt sad.

Everything smelled of
white paint and boxes.
Everything but the quilt.

So her mother rocked her
as mothers do.
Then tucked her in.
And she felt at home again
under the quilt.